PROBLEM SOLVING ON THE JOB

by Cynthia Benjamin

GLOBE FEARON EDUCATIONAL PUBLISHER
A Division of Simon & Schuster
Upper Saddle River, New Jersey

Executive Editor: Joan Carrafiello
Project Editors: Carol Schneider, Renée E. Beach
Editor: Bonnie Diamond, Ed. D.
Production Editor: Rosann Bar
Art Direction: Joan Jacobus
Interior Design: Paradigm Design, Inc.
Interior Art: Laurie Harden
Electronic Page Production: Paradigm Design, Inc.
Marketing: Margaret Rakus, Donna Frasco
Cover Illustration: Laurie Harden
Teacher Reviewers:

Carolyn Thalman
Special Education Teacher
Cleveland Middle School
Albuquerque, NM

Charlene Breh
Special Education Teacher
Corcoran High School
Syracuse, NY

Dr. Luann Purcell
Assistant Superintendent
Houston County Board of Education
Perry, GA

Printed in the United States of America

1 2 3 4 5 6 7 8 9 10   99 98 97 96

ISBN: 0-8359-3331-8

Contents

Introduction

What happens if you forget how to do a certain job at work? Suppose you don't get along with a co-worker? Where would you find the supply closet in your office? Everyone faces problems such as these on the job. In this book you will learn a simple way to solve problems.

Read the following "Problem Solving Plan." It lists four steps to follow when you have a problem.

Problem-Solving Plan

1. Understand

Ask yourself, "What is the problem? What do I need to find out?"

2. Plan and Solve

Ask yourself, "What do I already know? How will I solve this problem?" Then use a problem-solving skill to help you.

- ask a question such as "What if..."
- brainstorm
- compare
- decide
- discuss
- draw a picture or map
- estimate
- gather information
- look or observe
- make a list
- practice or try out
- read
- role-play
- talk to someone
- use mathematics skills
- work together
- write your ideas

Then carry out your plan.

3. Check

Look at what happened. Ask yourself, "Have I solved the problem? Does my plan make sense?" If there's still a problem, look over your plan. Change your plan. Try another problem-solving skill to solve the problem. Then try your new plan.

4. Review

Look at what you did to solve the problem.

Ask yourself, "What have I learned? How can I use my plan to solve problems like this in the future? Or can I solve a similar problem in a different way?"

In every lesson you will learn more about solving problems at work. If you have a problem, use this four-step "Problem-Solving Plan" to help you.

UNIT 1 PREPARING FOR WORK

How do you get ready for work every day?
What do you wear on your job?
How long does it take you to get to work?

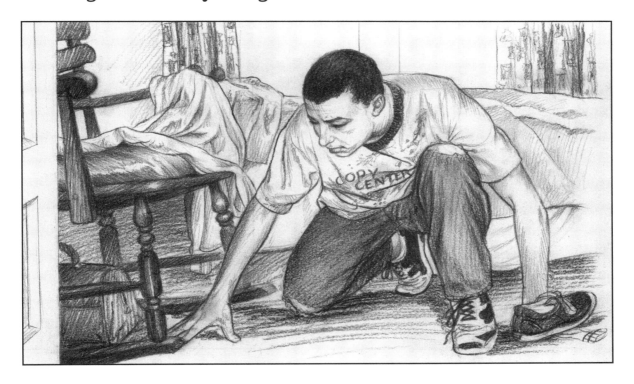

The lessons in this unit will help you learn about getting ready for work.

- In **Lesson 1**, you will meet Sam. He works at a copy shop. You'll find out how he gets ready for his job every morning.

- In **Lesson 2**, you'll find out how Sam decides what to wear to work.

- In **Lesson 3**, you'll learn how Sam gets to work.

What do you know about getting yourself ready for work?

_____

_____

_____

1 Getting Ready

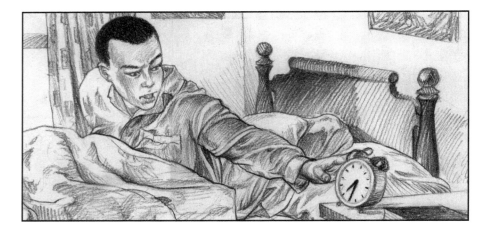

Sam woke up and looked at the clock. It was 7:30 A.M. He couldn't believe it! He was supposed to be up an hour ago. There were a million things to do before work. And he had forgotten to set the alarm. "Smart move, Sam," he thought.

Sam finished getting dressed. He ate breakfast quickly. Then he raced back to his bedroom. He had forgotten some papers for work. "Why didn't I get these papers together last night?" he thought. There was something else, too. This morning Sam was taking his niece to school. "I had better call my sister and tell her I'll be late," he thought.

It was going to be a busy morning. The school that Sam's niece went to was on West Fourth Street. Sam would have to take the bus to work from there. The bus ride would take an extra fifteen minutes.

"I'll never get to work by 8:30 now," Sam said to himself. "What am I going to do?"

1. Why will Sam be late for work?

_____

_____

2. What could Sam have done to plan ahead?

_____

_____

Discuss your answers with the other students in your group.

Thinking It Through

Sam didn't plan his time before leaving for work very well. There is a way he can help himself plan better.

- To **understand** his problem, Sam should ask himself a simple question: "What do I have to do before going to work?"

- To **plan** his time, Sam should write a personal schedule the night before. A **personal schedule** is a time plan. It tells you what to do and when to do it. Planning ahead helps you manage your time better.

- To **solve** his problem, Sam should follow his time plan. That way he would find out if his time plan worked.

- Sam should **check** his plan by following his personal schedule. That way he can find out if the plan works.

- Sam should **review** what he learned about managing his time. He should make any changes to his plan if he needs to. Reviewing his plan will help him better plan his time in the future.

Try This

Think about how Sam planned his time in the morning. Then role-play this scene:

You're getting ready for work. You woke up late and now you can't find your tote bag. Your workday starts at 9:00 A.M. It's already 8:45 A.M. As you're racing to the door, you remember something. You have to take a package to the post office before work.

Discuss your role-playing with the other students in your group. Use the following questions to help you:

1. What do you have to do before leaving for work?

2. Why is this a problem?

3. How can you solve the problem?

Remember

Make up a personal work schedule to help you better plan your time. Planning ahead is a good way to manage your time.

2 Getting Dressed

Sam grabbed his jacket and headed for the front door. He had to pick up his niece in ten minutes. Then he had to get to work at the copy shop...fast. "If I run all the way, I can make it," Sam thought. As he put on his jacket, he noticed his shirt. It was the same one he wore when he painted his room. The front of his shirt was covered with white paint. "I know Mr. Gonzalez won't like that," Sam thought. His boss wouldn't like his ripped jeans, either. Sam had meant to wash his work clothes the night before. But he forgot. Now there wasn't time to change.

Sam remembered what his boss said when he hired him.

"I want everyone at the copy shop to wear clean, neat clothes to work," Mr. Gonzalez had said.

"Just wait until he sees me," Sam thought. "I'm in big trouble today."

1. What was wrong with Sam's clothes?

_____

2. What do you think Sam's boss, Mr. Gonzalez, will do when Sam gets to work?

_____

_____

3. What would you do in Sam's place?

_____

_____

Discuss your answers with the other students in your group.

Thinking It Through

Sam knew he should dress a certain way for his job at the copy shop. This is called a **dress code**. His dirty shirt and torn jeans didn't fit the dress code for his job. Sam can make sure he wears the right work clothes in the future.

- Sam can **understand** that wearing the right work clothes is important. It shows he cares about his job.

- Sam can **plan** to **make a decision** about what he'll wear to work the night before. He can make sure his clothes are clean and neat. He can decide if they fit the dress code before getting dressed.

- Sam can **check** to make sure he has enough time to get dressed for work. He can wake up earlier to give himself enough time.

- Sam can **review** what he did to make sure he dressed the right way. He will learn how important it is to plan ahead.

Try This

Think about what you wear to work. Then role-play this scene:

> You work for the Parks Department in your community. On your job you wear a sweatshirt that says "Parks Department" on the front. You're supposed to wear a clean pair of jeans too. But you forgot to wash your work clothes last night. Your jeans are covered with mud. And you have to leave for work in ten minutes.

Discuss your role-playing with the other students in your group. Use the following questions to help you:

1. What should you have done before leaving for work?

2. How will you plan from now on?

3. Why would planning ahead have helped you solve the problem?

Remember

Be sure you wear the right clothes to work. Plan ahead so your work clothes are clean and neat.

---

3 Getting To Work

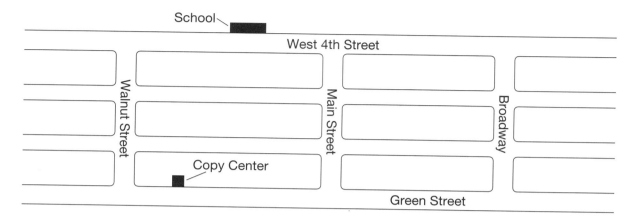

Sam had just dropped his niece at school on West Fourth Street. Now he had to get to the copy center on Green Street. Sam checked his watch. It was 8:15 A.M. He had to be at work by 8:30 A.M. Sam knew it would take him more time to get to work from his niece's school than from his home. The copy center was on the other side of town. There was only one problem. He wasn't sure how much time it would take.

"No problem," Sam said to himself. "I'll take the bus. No. Maybe the subway will be faster." But Sam didn't know which bus or subway to take. So he kept walking. While he walked he looked for a bus stop. The longer Sam walked, the more lost he became. He stopped and looked at his watch. It was 8:45 A.M. "Boy, am I going to be late," Sam thought. "If only I knew the fastest way to get to the copy center from here."

1. What are the problems Sam is having getting to work?

_____

_____

2. If you were in Sam's place, what would you do?

_____

_____

3. What could Sam have done so he didn't have this problem?

_____

_____

Discuss your answers with the other students in your group.

Thinking It Through

Sam had problems getting to work on time because he didn't plan ahead. There is a way he can help himself.

- Sam must **understand** what to do to get to work on time.

- Sam has to **plan** a route or way to get to the copy center from his niece's school. He should **write** these facts on a piece of paper:

  1. how to get to the copy center
  2. what bus or subway to take
  3. how long the trip will take

Then he should answer his questions by **drawing a map**.

- Sam should **check** his route by taking it to work. That way he can find out if it's a good route to take.

- After arriving at work, Sam should **review** what he learned. He can use the same steps to plan a route to another place.

Try This

Think about the problem Sam has in getting to work. Then role-play this scene:

> The store where you work has moved to a new address. You write down the address and telephone number. But you're not sure how to get there from your house. You walk to the nearest bus stop. The bus driver tells you to take the Number 2 bus. But you have to walk five blocks to the right bus stop. You're already late for work.

Discuss your role-playing with the other students in your group. Use the following questions to help you:

1. What could you do to find out how to get to the store?

2. What should you write on a piece of paper?

3. If you're going to be late to work, what should you do?

Remember
Always plan the route or how to get to work, how long it will take, and the way you will travel there.

UNIT 1 Review

In this unit you learned about

- preparing for work in the morning
- following a dress code for work
- getting to your job

Answer the following questions about the unit. Write your answers on the lines.

1. What is a personal schedule?

_____

_____

_____

_____

2. What is a dress code?

_____

_____

_____

_____

3. How should your work clothes always look when you leave in the morning?

_____

_____

_____

_____

4. What things should you think about to help you get to work on time?

_____

_____

_____

_____

5. Why is it important to plan ahead when you're getting ready for your job?

_____

_____

_____

_____

_____

_____

_____

_____

_____

_____

What if you were starting a new job tomorrow?

In your answer explain how you would get ready for work in the morning.

_____

_____

_____

_____

_____

_____

_____

_____

_____

_____

_____

_____

_____

Discuss your answers with other students in the class.

Journal

Think about what you learned in this unit.

1. This is what I learned about preparing for work.

_____

_____

_____

_____

2. These are the skills that were easy for me.

_____

_____

_____

_____

3. These are the skills I need to improve.

_____

_____

_____

_____

4. This is how I will improve these skills.

_____

_____

_____

_____

5. This is how I will use these skills to help prepare for work.

_____

_____

_____

_____

UNIT 2 MANAGING TIME

How do you manage your time every day?
How well do you plan your time at work?
How do you balance your time at work and at home?

The lessons in this unit will help you learn to manage your time.

- In **Lesson 4**, you will meet Ellen. She works as a stock clerk. You'll find out why it's important for her to be on time.

- In **Lesson 6**, you'll learn how Ellen plans her work time.

- In **Lesson 5**, you'll find out why it's important for Ellen to understand what her workday means.

- In **Lesson 7**, you'll learn how Ellen balances her work time and her personal life.

What do you know about about managing your time?

_____

_____

_____

4 Being on Time

Ellen looked at her watch at the bus stop. It was 8:45 A.M. She had to be at work by 9:00 A.M. "That's great," Ellen thought to herself. "I should be at work in fifteen minutes." When Ellen got off the bus, it was 8:55. It took her only a few minutes to walk to her job. Ellen was a stock clerk in a big store. When she arrived at work, Ellen's watch said 9:00 A.M. Then she slipped her **time card** into the digital time clock. Her time card showed the exact times when Ellen arrived at work and left work. But the digital time clock read 9:05 A.M. So the time on Ellen's time card was 9:05 A.M. too. "Now my boss will be mad at me because I'm late. And I won't be paid for a full hour of work," Ellen said to herself.

1. Why was Ellen late for work?

_____

_____

2. What will happen when Ellen is late?

_____

_____

3. What would you do in Ellen's place?

_____

_____

Discuss your answers with the other students in your group.

Thinking It Through

Ellen was late to work. Ellen's watch was slower than the time clock at work. She didn't leave herself enough time. There is a way she can avoid being late in the future.

- Ellen should **understand** what her problem is. She can ask herself: "Why am I late for work?" Ellen should understand that she was late because she cut the margin too close.

- Ellen should **plan** to have more time than she needs to get to work on time. She should plan to be early. Many things can happen that can cause her to be late to work.

- To **solve** her problem Ellen can set her watch according to the time clock at work and allow herself extra time to get to work.

- She can **check** and make sure that she doesn't cut the margin so close in the future.

- Ellen can **review** what she learned about being on time. Reviewing will help her solve similar problems in the future.

Try This

Think about the reason that Ellen was late for work. Then act out this scene:

> When you get to work, you put your time card in the time clock. Your boss is angry because you're late. He warns you not to be late again. You try to explain that you got caught in an accident. He doesn't want to listen to any excuses.

Discuss your role-playing with the other students in your group. Use the following questions to help you:

1. What could you do so you won't be late for work again?

2. What will you say to your boss?

3. Do you think he should be angry with you for being late?

Remember

Make sure you plan to have extra time to get to work. Check to be sure that your watch has the correct time.

---

5 Your Workday

On the way to the stockroom Ellen stopped at the store cafeteria. She had left her house without having breakfast. "It will just take a few minutes to get a roll and a cup of coffee," she thought. "Besides, I'm already late. Ten more minutes won't matter." When Ellen was leaving the cafeteria, she saw her friend Denise. The two friends made plans to go shopping at lunch. "We can take an extra fifteen minutes on our lunch hour," Ellen said. By the time she reached the stockroom it was 9:45 A.M. All the other stock clerks were already at work.

1. Why was Ellen late to the stockroom?

_____

_____

2. Do you think Ellen should have stopped for breakfast? Explain.

_____

_____

3. How do you think Ellen's co-workers felt when she was late?

_____

_____

Discuss your answers with the other students in your group.

Thinking It Through

Ellen's **workday** is the number of hours she must work every day. Her workday begins and ends at certain times. Ellen had a problem because she did not follow her workday hours. She did not act responsibly.

- Ellen must **understand** how important it is to be on time for work, to work until the end of the day, and to take only the time the job allows for lunch.

- Ellen must **plan** her time better. She should have breakfast before leaving for work. She can't take extra time during her lunch.

- Ellen should **check** her watch during her workday. That way she can manage her time better.

- Then Ellen should **review** what she learned about being on time. It will help her plan her lunch and work breaks too.

Try This

Think about being on time at work. Then act out this scene:

> You have one hour for lunch and you want to go shopping. You leave work at 12:15 P.M. and you plan to return by 1:15 P.M. By the time you finish shopping, it's almost 1:30 P.M. And you still haven't had any lunch!

Talk about your role-playing with the other students in your group. Use the following questions to help you:

1. Should you plan to go shopping on your lunch time? Explain.

2. Why is it important to take the correct amount of time for lunch?

3. How could you have planned your time better? What could you have done differently? Explain.

Remember

Get to work on time in the morning. Don't take extra time during your lunch or breaks.

---

6 Organizing Work Time

Invoice

No.	Item	Price	Total
3	blue skirt	17.95	53.85
3	beige blouse	10.99	32.97
4	print blouse	9.99	39.96

Ellen started unpacking the six boxes of skirts and blouses for her department. Then she had to check the invoice for each box. An **invoice** is a detailed list of goods and their prices. Ellen wasn't sure how long it would take to complete both jobs.

While she was working, her boss, Ms. Gomez, came up to her.

"Ellen, will you be finished by lunchtime?" Ms. Gomez asked. "We're expecting another delivery this afternoon."

Ellen nodded. "No problem." But the next time Ellen looked at her watch it was almost time for lunch. And she still had two more boxes to unpack. Then she had to check all the invoices.

1. What were the two jobs that Ellen had to do?

_____

_____

2. Why did Ellen's boss want to be sure Ellen would be finished by lunchtime?

_____

3. Should Ellen have told her boss that she would be finished by lunch? Explain.

_____

_____

Discuss your answers with the other students in your group.

Thinking It Through

Ellen didn't organize her work time very well. There is a way she can help herself.

- To **understand** her problem, Ellen should ask herself two questions:

    1. What are the jobs I have to do?

    2. How much time will each job take?

- Ellen should **plan** her time at work. She can **estimate** how long each job will take. Last week she spent one hour unpacking two boxes and checking the invoices. This week she has more to do, so it will take her more time than it did last week. It might take her about three hours to unpack all six boxes.

- After Ellen finished her work, she should **check** to see how long she spent on both jobs.

- Ellen should **review** what she learned about organizing her time at work. This will help her plan her time in the future.

Try This

Think about how Ellen organized her time at work. Then act out this scene:

> You are a stock clerk in a supermarket. You have ten large boxes of canned food to unpack by 4:00 P.M. You started the job at 2:00 P.M. It's now 3:00 P.M. You've only unpacked four of the boxes. Your boss tells you that another shipment just arrived. He wants to know if you can help out.

Discuss your role-playing with the other students in your group. Use the following questions to help you:

1. What questions can you ask yourself to help plan your time?

2. What should you tell your boss when he asks you to help out?

Remember

Understand what job or jobs you have to do. Then decide how much time you'll spend on each job. Don't say you can do something unless you will be able to finish it.

7 Work Time and Personal Life

It was 4:45 P.M. Ellen's work day was over at 5:00 P.M. But today Ellen had a special problem. She had to pick up her two-year old daughter, Serena, at her mother's house by 5:15 P.M. That meant she needed to leave work early. Ellen had worked hard all afternoon. She had unpacked the boxes and checked the invoices. "No one will care if I leave work fifteen minutes early," she thought. "My baby is more important than this job. Besides, what's going to happen so late in the day?"

But a few minutes after Ellen left, her boss, Ms. Gomez, came into the stockroom. "Has anyone seen Ellen?" Ms. Gomez asked one of the clerks. "I need to talk to her."

1. Why did Ellen leave work early?

_____

_____

2. Why did Ellen think it was all right to leave work early?

_____

_____

3. If you were Ellen, what would you have done?

_____

_____

Discuss your answers with the other students in your group.

Thinking It Through

Ellen had a problem managing her work time and her personal time. There is a way she can solve it.

- Ellen can **understand** what her problem is. She has to pick up her daughter at a certain time. To do that, Ellen has to leave work early. She is supposed to stay on her job until the end of the workday.

- Ellen can **plan** a way to **solve** her problem. She can **make** a list of the people who can help her and she can **talk** to them. These people are her mother and her boss. This will help Ellen plan ahead. Ellen can ask her mother to baby-sit a little longer at the end of the day. If her mother says no, then Ellen can ask her boss to let her leave work fifteen minutes early.

- Ellen can **check** to see if she solved the problem. She can ask herself: "What did my mother say? What did my boss say"?

- Ellen can **review** the way she managed her work time and her personal time. She will learn how important it is to plan ahead.

Try This

Think about how you manage your work time and your personal time. Then act out this scene:

> You have to see your doctor right away. You call her office to make an appointment. But the only time she can see you is tomorrow at 9:15 A.M. You have to be at work by 9:00 A.M. What should you do?

Discuss your role-playing with the other students in your group. Use the following questions to help you:

1. Will you see your doctor at 9:15 A.M.?

2. What will you say to your boss if you make the appointment?

3. What could you have done differently so you would not have this problem?

Remember

It's important to balance your work time and your personal time. If there is a problem, plan ahead.

UNIT 2 Review

In this unit you learned about

- being on time

- what a workday is

- planning your time at work

- managing your work time and your personal time

Answer the following questions about the unit. Write your answers on the lines.

1. Why should you plan to be early to work?

_____

_____

_____

_____

_____

2. What is a workday?

_____

3. What can you do to help plan your work time?

_____

_____

_____

_____

_____

4. If you have problems managing your work time and your personal time, what can you do?

_____

_____

_____

_____

_____

5. Describe how you will be better at planning your time at work.

_____

_____

_____

_____

_____

_____

_____

_____

_____

_____

_____

What if you will be late returning to work after lunch?

You have a doctor's appointment during your lunch hour. When you get to the doctor's office, you find out that the doctor can't see you for another fifteen minutes. Explain your answer.

_____

_____

_____

_____

_____

_____

_____

_____

_____

_____

Discuss your answers with other students in the class.

Journal

Think about what you learned in this unit.

1. This is what I learned about managing my time at work.

_____

_____

_____

_____

2. This is what I'm not sure about.

_____

_____

_____

_____

3. These are the time-planning skills I have to improve.

_____

_____

_____

_____

4. This is how I will improve these time-planning skills.

_____

_____

_____

_____

5. This is why it's important to plan my time better at work.

_____

_____

_____

_____

UNIT 3 MANAGING JOB DUTIES

Do you know what you're supposed to do at work?
Do you finish the most important job first?
Do you complete your job tasks on time?

The lessons in this unit will help you learn about your responsibilities at work.

- In **Lesson 8**, you'll meet Tara. You'll find out how Tara fills in forms.

- In **Lesson 9**, you'll find out how Tara learns about her job duties.

- In **Lesson 10**, you'll find out why Tara finishes the most important job task first.

- In **Lesson 11**, you'll learn how Tara finishes her job tasks on time.

- In **Lesson 12**, you'll find out how Tara dresses for her job.

- In **Lesson 13**, you'll learn how Tara finds out important information where she works.

How well are you managing your job duties now? What are they?

_____

_____

8 Completing Forms

```
┌──────────────────────────────────────────────────────────────────┐
│                        Information Form                            │
│   ──────────────────────────────────────────────────────────      │
│   Please Print                                                     │
│   1. Name_____    2. S.S._____   │
│   3. Address_____    City_____ State___ Zip___│
│   4. Phone_____    5. School_____    │
│   6. Mother's Name_____    Address_____    │
│   7. Father's Name_____    Address_____    │
│   8. Contact in case of emergency:                                 │
│      Name_____                                 │
│      Name_____                                 │
└──────────────────────────────────────────────────────────────────┘
```

Tara had just started working part-time at her neighborhood library. Her boss, Mr. Lee, gave her a form to complete. "This form tells us information about you, such as your address and phone number," he said. "Please fill in all the blanks. We will need this form for our records."

Tara wasn't sure what to write in some of the blanks. Mr. Lee needed the form back by lunchtime. Tara worked in the children's reading room all morning. A few minutes before her lunch break, she looked at the form again. Tara was in a hurry to complete it. She left some lines blank. "I can fill those in some other time," she thought. Tara crossed out a lot of words, too. Her handwriting wasn't very clear. Tara wrote in script. After she finished, she noticed a line at the top of the form. It said, "Please print."

1. What mistakes did Tara make as she filled in the form?

_____

_____

2. How could Tara have found out what to print in the blanks?

_____

_____

3. Since Tara didn't have enough time to complete the form, what could she have done?

_____

Discuss your answers with the other students in your group.

Thinking It Through

Completing forms correctly is an important job skill. Sometimes workers must fill in **applications forms** when they look for work. Or they have to fill in other types of forms for their job. Tara filled in an information form at the library. She made some mistakes. But there is a way she can help herself.

- To **understand** what to do, Tara can ask: What do I have to do to complete this form?

- To **plan** and **solve** her problems, Tara should read the form first before starting to fill it in. Then she can make a list of what she has to do to complete it.

> 1. I must answer all the questions.
>
> 2. I need to find more information for some of the questions.
>
> 3. I have to complete the form neatly and correctly.
>
> 4. I need more time to fill in the form.

Then she can reread her list. She can do some of these things herself. She will have to **ask** her boss for more time. Also, she must ask him to explain some questions on the form.

When Tara has read the form thoroughly and done everything on her list, she will be ready to fill in the form.

- Now, Tara should **check** the information she wrote on the form. She should make sure she did not make any careless mistakes.

- Tara should **review** what she learned about completing forms. She can use these skills in the future.

Remember

It's important to fill in work forms completely and neatly. Always follow the directions on the form. If you don't know what to do, ask for help. Asking for help shows that you want to do the right thing.

9 Job Duties

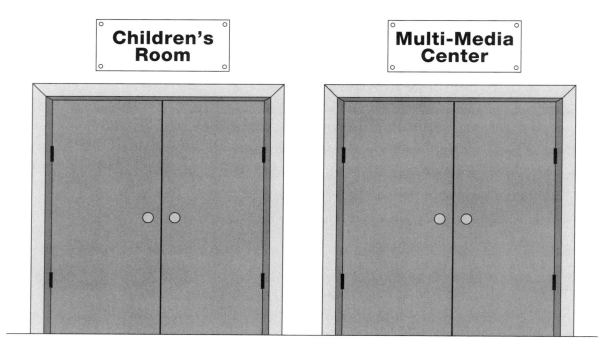

Children's Room

Multi-Media Center

Tara worked part-time at the library. On Tuesdays, Tara worked at the desk where people returned their library books. Then, after her work break, Tara put away magazines in the reading room. Today, Tara's boss, Mr. Lee, asked her to help put back video tapes on the shelves. Tara wasn't sure what she should do. Should she put away magazines or put away the video tapes?

1. What are Tara's job duties at the library on Tuesdays?

_____

_____

2. Why is Tara feeling unsure about about what to do?

_____

_____

3. If you were Tara, what would you do?

_____

_____

Discuss your answers with the other students in your group.

Thinking It Through

It's important to understand what your **job duties** are. Job duties are the different tasks you do on your job. Good workers finish all the jobs they are given. Tara isn't sure what she has to do.

- Tara can **understand** what her problem is. She can ask herself: What is it that I don't understand? Tara doesn't know what her job duties are.

- To **plan** and **solve** her problem, Tara can write down her job duties on a piece of paper. Then she can ask her boss what she should do next. She can add his answer to her list of job duties.

- After completing her job duties, Tara can **check** and **review** what she learned. Today she learned that it's okay to ask her boss to explain something again. The next time Mr. Lee asks Tara to do several tasks, she should list the job duties in a small note pad or calendar. She should keep a pad and pen with her daily to be able to write down important information.

Try This

Think about how you handle your job duties. Then role-play this scene:

> You work in a pizza restaurant. Your boss wants you to do three job tasks today. You finish sweeping the restaurant. But you don't know what to do next. What should you do?

Discuss your role-playing with the other students in your group. Use the following questions to help you:

1. When your boss gives you a list of job tasks, what should you do?

2. If you forget what to do on your job, whom can you ask for help?

3. What are some things that you should definitely not do? Explain.

--- **Remember** ---

It's important to know what your job duties are and to complete each one. If you forget what to do, ask for help.

10 Planning Which Job to Do First

Tara was really busy at work. First, she started to help the librarian check in the videotapes. Next, her boss, Mr. Lee, asked Tara to put some new children's books away. The job was important and would take several hours. It had to be finished by the end of the day. Tara started unpacking the new books right away. Then, Danny, another library worker, needed help at the book return desk. He asked Tara to help him out. "It will only take twenty minutes. You can finish putting the books away later." Tara wasn't sure which job to do first. She decided to help her friend Danny. After she helped Danny, she took her work break.

1. What was the most important job that Tara had to do? Explain why you think it was the most important job.

_____

_____

_____

_____

2. What do you think of Tara's decision to help Danny?

_____

_____

_____

_____

Discuss your answers with the other students in your group.

Thinking It Through

Tara had three different jobs to do. She wasn't sure which job to do first. Then, after doing one job, she took a work break. But Tara can manage her job duties better in the future.

- Tara can **understand** her problem. She can ask herself: "Which job should I do first? next? last?

- To **plan** a way to **solve** her problem, Tara can list the three jobs she has to do. Then she should **gather information** about each job. That will help her decide which job to do first. Tara's boss asked her to put away the children's books. That job will take a long time. It had to be finished by the end of the day. Tara should do that job first. Then she should go on to the next most important job—helping the librarian. Last, Tara should help her friend, Danny.

- After following her plan, Tara should **check** what she did. She can ask herself: Did I do the most important job first? Did I go to the next job right away until I finished all my work?

- Tara should **review** what she did. She can use the same plan the next time she has several jobs to do.

Try This

Think about the different jobs Tara had to do. Then act out this scene:

> Your boss asked you to deliver a package to a customer right away. You also have to unpack boxes in the stockroom. Then a friend asks you to pick up lunch for everyone in the stockroom.

Discuss your role-playing with the other students in your group. Use the following questions to help you:

1. Which job is most important to do first, and why?

2. Which job should you do second? third? last?

3. After finishing one job, what should you do right away?

Remember

Do the most important job first. After you complete one job, go on to the next job right away.

---

11 Completing Jobs on Time

Tara went back to work putting the new books away after her break. Her boss, Mr. Lee, wanted the job done by the end of the day. But Tara had taken time to help her friend at the return desk. There were a lot of new children's books to put away, too. Tara looked at her watch. It was 4:30 P.M. Tara knew she wouldn't finish her task by 5:00 P.M. Then Mr. Lee stopped by the children's reading room. "How are things going, Tara? Will you be finished by 5:00 P.M.?"

Tara gulped. "Sure, Mr. Lee. No problem." After he left, Tara looked at the boxes of books. "What am I going to do now?" she thought to herself.

1. Why didn't Tara have enough time to finish her job?

_____

_____

2. Why did Tara tell her boss she would have the job finished by 5:00 P.M.?

_____

_____

3. If you were Tara, what would you have said to your boss?

_____

_____

Discuss your answers with the other students in your group.

Thinking It Through

It's important to finish your job tasks on time. If you can't, talk to your boss and explain the problem. Here's how Tara can handle her problem.

- Tara must **understand** what the problem is. She has to finish putting the books on the shelves by 5:00. She won't finish the job in time.

- To **plan** and **solve** the problem, Tara should **estimate** how much time she'll need to put away the rest of the books. Then, she should **talk** to her boss and explain the problem. First, she should tell him how much more time it will take to finish the job. Then she should tell him when the job will be finished. Finally she should complete the job as soon as she can.

- Tara should **check** her plan and make sure she put away all the books.

- Finally, Tara should **review** what she learned about completing jobs on time. That way, she will be able to use what she learned to help her solve similar problems in the future.

Try This

Think about how well you manage your job tasks. Then act out this scene:

> You are a messenger. Your boss asks you to deliver a package by 5:00 P.M. But you can't find the address. By the time you find the right address, the business is closed for the day. What should you do?

Discuss your role-playing with the other students in your group. Use the following questions to help you:

1. What should you do if you can't finish a job on time?

2. Why should you tell your boss?

3. What did you learn by role-playing this scene?

Remember

Always try to finish a job on time. If there's a problem, talk to your boss about it.

---

12 Dressing for Work

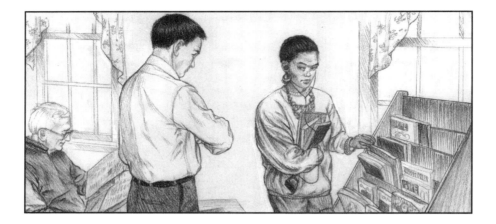

It was a rainy day, so Tara decided to wear her old jeans and a sweatshirt to work at the library. Her jeans were torn, but she didn't care. Tara brought her radio to work, too. Since she was wearing earphones, the music wouldn't bother anyone, she thought. When Tara walked into the library, her friend, Michelle, stopped her.

"Great earrings," Michelle said.

"Thanks," Tara answered. "I like wearing fancy jewelry sometimes. That's why I tried out the new eye shadow, too. What do you think?"

"I think you're the foxiest girl here," Michelle said.

Tara put on her earphones and turned on her radio. Then she started returning the magazines to the shelves. Her boss, Mr. Lee, wanted to talk to Tara about her work. But she couldn't hear him because she was wearing her earphones. So Mr. Lee tapped Tara on the shoulder. Then he pointed to her torn jeans.

1. Why did Tara wear old jeans and a sweatshirt to her job?

_____

_____

2. What was Tara wearing that wasn't right for her library job?

_____

_____

_____

Discuss your answers with the other students in your group.

Thinking It Through

Every job has a **dress code**. A dress code is a special way of dressing for a certain job. Tara didn't look the right way for her job at the library. She can plan to wear the proper work clothes from now on.

- Tara can **understand** the problem. She can ask herself, "What is the dress code at my job? Am I following the dress code?"

- Tara can **plan** how to **solve** her problem. She needs to know the dress code. To find out, she can **look** at the way the other library workers dress and look. She can ask herself: "Do they wear heavy makeup? Do they wear a lot of jewelry? Do they bring their radios and headsets to work and listen to them on the job?" If she still has questions, she can also **ask** one of her co-workers or one of the librarians about the dress code.

- Then Tara can follow the dress code. She can **check** to see if her plan worked.

- Tara can **review** what she learned about looking the right way for her job.

Try This

Think about how Tara solved her problem. Then act out this scene:

> You have been working at the shoe store for a week. One day you wear your old jeans and a torn T-shirt. The next day you wear a fancy sweater and lots of jewelry. But you still don't look right for your job. What should you do?

Discuss your role-playing with the other students in your group. Use the following questions to help you:

1. What is a good way to find out the dress code for your job?

2. Why is it important to follow the dress code for your job?

3. What did you learn from your role-playing?

> ### Remember
>
> It's important to dress the right way for your job. Following the dress code shows your boss that your job is important to you.

13 Finding Information

Tara needed labels for the new cassettes and videos. Her boss, Mr. Lee, asked her to get the labels from the supply room. Tara had only been working at the library for a short time. She still wasn't sure where some things were located. Tara thought the supply room was on the third floor. She looked there first. Tara couldn't find the supply room there. Then she looked at her watch. It was almost 4:00. Her boss wanted the job finished by 4:30 and Tara still didn't have the labels.

1. What information did Tara need?

_____

_____

2. Why couldn't Tara find the supply room?

_____

_____

3. If you were Tara, what would you have done?

_____

_____

Discuss your answers with the other students in your group.

Thinking It Through

It's important to know how to find information you will need for your job. Tara couldn't find the supply room. There is a way to solve her problem.

- Tara should **understand** what her problem is. She doesn't know where the supply room in the library is located.

- Tara should **plan** and **solve** her problem. To do that she has to **gather information** she needs. Tara has to find out where the supply closet is located. The best way to find out is by **asking** a co-worker or her boss, Mr. Lee. Then she can **write** down where the supply room is or draw a map to show where it is. That will help Tara remember how to find it in the future.

- Tara can **check** what she did to make sure she solved her problem.

- Tara can **review** what she learned about finding information. That way she can solve similar problems in the future.

Try This

Think about how Tara found the information she needed. Then act out this scene:

> You have been working at your job in the department store for two days. It's lunchtime. You agreed to meet two of your co-workers in the lunchroom. You thought the lunchroom was on the second floor of the building. It isn't. What should you do?

Discuss your role-playing with the other students in your group. Use the following questions to help you:

1. What information do you need?

2. What's the best way of getting that information?

3. What did you learn from your role-playing?

Remember

If you aren't sure how to find things at work, ask your boss or a co-worker to help you.

UNIT 3 Review

In this unit you learned about

- completing forms at work

- knowing your job duties

- doing the most important job first

- finishing a job on time

- following the dress code for your job

- finding information you'll need for your job

Answer the following questions about the unit. Write your answers on the lines.

1. What should you do when you complete a form at work?

_____

_____

_____

2. If you aren't sure about your job duties, whom should you ask?

_____

_____

_____

3. What kind of clothes should you wear to work?

_____

_____

_____

_____

4. If you aren't sure where the elevator is at work, whom should you ask?

_____

_____

_____

_____

5. Why is it important to put jobs in order and do the most
important job first? Why is it important to go on to the next
job after finishing the first one?

_____

_____

_____

_____

_____

_____

_____

_____

_____

What if you have two different jobs to do at work. Which job would you do first and why?

Your boss has told you that clearing out the stockroom
is the most important job to do. You also have to deliver
a package to a customer. Explain.

_____

_____

_____

_____

_____

_____

_____

_____

_____

_____

_____

_____

Discuss your answers with other students in the class.

Journal

Think about what you learned in this unit.

1. This is what I learned about managing my job duties.

_____

_____

_____

_____

2. This is what I'm still not sure about managing my job duties.

_____

_____

_____

_____

3. These are the skills about managing my job duties that I want to improve.

_____

_____

_____

_____

4. This is how I will improve these skills so I can better manage my job duties.

_____

_____

_____

_____

5. This is what I learned when acting out the role-playing scenes in this unit.

_____

_____

_____

_____

UNIT 4 COMMUNICATION SKILLS

**How do you talk to your boss? your co-workers?
What do you do if your boss says "Great job!" or
"You made a mistake!"?**

The lessons in this unit will help you learn about talking
to people at work.

- In **Lesson 14**, you'll meet Tommy. He works at a supermarket. You'll find out how he talks to his boss.

- In **Lesson 15**, you'll learn how Tommy talks to his co-workers.

- In **Lesson 16**, you'll learn how Tommy talks to his customers.

- In **Lesson 17**, you'll find out how Tommy acts when his boss praises and complains about his work.

- In **Lesson 18**, you'll learn how Tommy asks questions to learn how to do his job.

What problem do you have talking to different people at work?

_____

_____

14 Talking with a Boss

When Tommy arrived at the supermarket, his boss, Ms. Wong, wanted to talk to him. Ms. Wong was changing Tommy's work schedule. She wanted to be sure that Tommy understood his new schedule. While Ms. Wong talked, Tommy kept his hands in his pockets. He looked down at his feet. He was waiting for Ms. Wong to finish talking. While he waited, Tommy wasn't really listening to Ms. Wong. He just wanted a chance to talk himself. Finally Ms. Wong said, "Tommy, please look at me. I don't think you've heard a word I said." Then Tommy looked up at his boss. "Do you understand your new schedule?" Ms. Wong asked.

Tommy just shrugged. "What new schedule?"

1. How did Tommy act when his boss talked to him?

_____

_____

2. Why didn't Tommy listen to what his boss was saying?

_____

_____

3. How do you think Ms.Wong felt about Tommy's actions? Why do you think she felt this way?

_____

_____

Discuss your answers with the other students in your group.

Thinking It Through

Having a conversation means listening to what another person says and answering. Tommy had a problem talking to his boss. There is a way he can help himself.

- Tommy has to **understand** his problem. He can ask himself, "What problem am I having talking with Ms. Wong?" Tommy has to recognize what his **body language** was saying to Ms. Wong. Body language is the way you look and act when you talk or listen. Good body language is looking at the speaker, standing straight and still, making notes, if necessary.

- Tommy can **plan** a way to **solve** his problem. He can practice his body language by looking into a mirror and by watching other people as they listen. How you look at someone is just as important as what you say. Tommy can listen to what his boss says before he answers.

- Tommy can **check** his plan for solving his problem. When his boss talks to him, Tommy can follow his plan. Then he can see if his plan works.

- Tommy can **review** what he learned about talking to his boss. He can use his plan whenever he talks to his boss or anyone else at work.

Try This

Think about how Tommy acted when his boss talked to him. Then act out this scene with another student:

Your boss is asking you a question about a telephone order that you took. While he talks, you aren't really listening. Your body language shows you aren't paying attention to him. Then he asks you a question. You don't know what to say.

Discuss your role-playing with the other students in your group. Use the following questions to help you:

1. How will you show that you aren't really listening to your boss?

2. How will your boss act when he knows you aren't paying attention?

Remember

When you have a conversation with your boss, listen to what is said. Use good body language, too.

15 Talking with Co-Workers

Tommy was helping another worker, José, arrange cans of food in the store. "Do you think we should put a sign above the cans?" José asked. "That way the customers will know how much each can costs." Tommy wasn't listening to José, so he didn't answer him.

José put the sign above the cans of food. Then Tommy noticed the sign. "That looks really dumb," he said to José. "You can't even read the prices. Boy, what a stupid idea."

1. Why didn't Tommy answer José's question?

_____

_____

2. When Tommy saw the sign, how did he react?

_____

_____

3. How do you think José felt when Tommy said José's idea was stupid?

_____

_____

_____

Discuss your answers with the other students in your group.

Thinking It Through

Tommy had a problem talking to his co-worker, José.
There is a way he can solve his problem.

- Tommy has to **understand** his problem. He can ask himself, "What did I do wrong?" Tommy didn't listen to his co-worker, José. A **co-worker** is a person you work with on your job. Also, Tommy didn't treat José with respect.

- Tommy can **plan** a way to **solve** his problem. He can **ask** himself, **What if** I talked to a co-worker and he didn't listen to me? **What if** a co-worker said my idea was dumb or stupid? That way Tommy can understand how José feels. If Tommy doesn't like José's idea, he can work with José to brainstorm another idea.

- Tommy can **check** his plan the next time he talks to a co-worker.

- Then Tommy can **review** what he learned about talking to his co-workers. That way he can solve similar problems in the future.

Try This

Think about how Tommy talked to José. Then act out this scene with other students in your group:

> Your boss asks you and your co-worker Diane to deliver several packages. You and Diane have to plan which packages to deliver. Diane wants to deliver the packages to Green Street first. You don't like her idea.

Discuss your role-playing with the other students in your group. Use the following questions to help you:

1. Did you listen to what Diane said before talking?

2. Did you brainstorm another plan to deliver the packages?

3. What did you learn from your role-playing?

┌─ **Remember** ─────────────────────────────
Listen to what co-workers say. If you disagree with a
co-worker, try to brainstorm another way of handling
the problem.
└───

16 Talking with Customers

Mr. Malone wanted his groceries delivered to his home by 1:00 P.M. Tommy's boss, Ms. Wong, asked Tommy to deliver the order. Tommy wanted to do a good job. He made sure that he arrived at Mr. Malone's house on time. Then Mr. Malone asked Tommy to carry the heavy bags into the kitchen and put them on the table. Mr. Malone watched Tommy carry in the bags. He didn't thank Tommy or give him a tip. Then Mr. Malone said, "The next time I want these groceries delivered on time."

Tommy got mad. "Are you crazy? I was here by 1:00," he said to Mr. Malone.

"Don't talk back to me," Mr. Malone yelled.

As Tommy left Mr. Malone's house, he slammed the door. Then he kicked it.

1. How do you think Mr. Malone treated Tommy?

_____

_____

2. Put yourself in Tommy's place. What would you have said to Mr. Malone?

_____

_____

Discuss your answers with the other students in your group.

Thinking It Through

Mr. Malone was mean to Tommy. But that doesn't give Tommy the right to yell or kick his door. Tommy can handle the problem in another way.

- Tommy can **understand** what the problem is. He can ask himself, "What can I say and do when I have a difficult customer?"

- Tommy can **plan** how to **solve** his problem. When Tommy returns to the supermarket, he can **role play** with a co-worker how to talk to a difficult customer. Tommy must learn not to yell or get angry. He should explain what happened and use a polite voice when talking to a customer.

  Tommy can **practice** speaking in front of a mirror, too. He should make sure that he uses polite words. That way when he is facing a difficult customer, the right words will come easily to him.

- Tommy can **check** his plan the next time he has a difficult customer to deal with.

- Tommy can **review** what he learned about talking to customers.

Try This

Think about how Tommy talked to and acted toward Mr. Malone. Then act out this scene:

> You are taking an order from a customer on the telephone. You are talking to the customer politely. But the customer starts to yell at you. What do you do?

Discuss your role-playing with the other students in your group. Use the following questions to help you:

1. How should you talk and act to a difficult customer?

2. If the customer complains about you to your boss, what should you do?

3. Have you ever had a customer like Mr. Malone? What did you do?

┌─ **Remember** ─────────────────────────────
│ Always talk politely to a customer. Never yell or get
│ angry so the customer sees.
└──

17 Listening

Tommy was late coming back from his work break. His boss, Ms. Wong, called him aside. "Tommy, this is the third time you've been late in two weeks. I want you to be on time from now on."

Tommy frowned. Then he looked down at the floor. "Yeah, sure," he said in a low voice. But Ms. Wong couldn't even hear him. When Ms. Wong left, Tommy sat down. "Boy, everything I do around here is wrong."

A few days later, Tommy was waiting for a package to deliver to Mr. Chin. Ms. Wong smiled at him. "Thanks for working late last night," she said. "And you did a really good job, too." Tommy just nodded. He didn't say anything. When Ms.Wong went into her office, Tommy grinned. He felt really proud. He felt so good that he stopped working for half an hour.

1. What was Tommy's body language like when his boss told him not to be late?

_____

_____

2. If you were Tommy, what would you have done when Ms. Wong said that you did a good job?

_____

_____

Discuss your answers with the other students in your group.

Thinking It Through

Tommy wasn't sure how to act when his boss told him not to be late any more. Later, he didn't know what to say when his boss praised his work. There is a way he can help himself.

- Tommy can **understand** his problem. He doesn't know how to act when his boss likes his work and when his boss doesn't like his work.

- Tommy can **plan** a way to **solve** his problem. He can **practice** in front of a mirror how he should look at his boss and how to answer her in a clear, firm voice. He can learn to say "Thank you" if his boss praises him. He can learn to go back to his job right away. Then Tommy can use his plan when his boss talks to him.

- Tommy can **check** the way he acts when Ms. Wong talks about his work.

- Tommy can **review** what he learned.

Try This

Think about how Tommy acted when his boss talked about his work. Then act out this scene:

> You work at a parking garage. One of your co-workers didn't come to work today. You've been doing his job, too. It's been a really busy day, so you didn't take a lunch break. Your boss thanks you for all your hard work. In his next breath, he yells at you because you forgot to wash a customer's car. What should you do?

Discuss your role-playing with the other students in your group. Use the following questions to help you:

1. How did you look and act when your boss said he liked your work?

2. How did you look and act when your boss yelled at you?

3. What did you say to your boss?

Remember

If your boss praises your work, always say thank you. If your boss doesn't like your work, listen carefully. Then answer your boss in a firm, clear voice.

---

18 Asking Questions

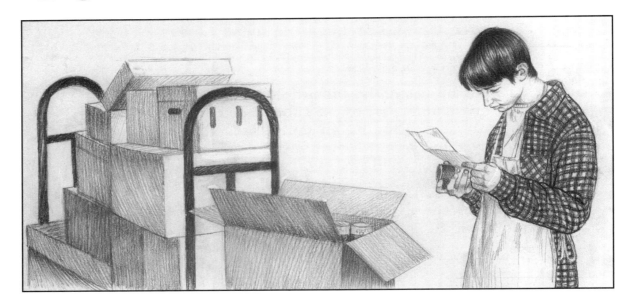

One of Tommy's jobs was checking the forms for each shipment of food. These forms are called invoices. Tommy hadn't checked an invoice in a long time. He was unpacking four boxes of canned food. Ms.Wong wanted Tommy to check the invoice for the shipment. Tommy looked at the form. His boss had explained the form to Tommy before. He couldn't remember what the different numbers meant. Tommy felt funny about asking Ms. Wong to explain the form again. So he tried to do the job without help. After an hour Tommy still wasn't sure what to do.

1. Why didn't Tommy understand how to check the form?

_____

_____

2. Why didn't Tommy ask his boss to explain the form again?

_____

_____

3. If you were Tommy, what would you have done?

_____

_____

Discuss your answers with the other students in your group.

Thinking It Through

It's all right to ask your boss or a co-worker questions if you need help. Tommy didn't want to ask Ms. Wong how to read the form. But there is a way he can help himself.

- Tommy can **understand** his problem. He can ask himself: "How can I learn to read this form for my job?"

- Tommy can **plan** how to **solve** his problem. He can **list his questions** about how to read the form. Then he can ask his boss the questions. Tommy should talk to Ms. Wong politely and in a clear voice. Next, he can **write** down the answers to his questions. Finally, he can use the information when he reads the invoices.

- Tommy can **check** his plan. Can he use the information to read the invoice? If he can, then Tommy's plan is a good one.

- Tommy can **review** what he learned about asking questions. Now he can ask questions whenever he has a problem or needs help.

Try This

Think about how Tommy asked his boss questions about his job. Then act out this scene:

> You have to call a customer about an order. But you can't find the customer's telephone number. You know your boss has a file of all the customers' names and telephone numbers. But you don't know where the file is or how to use it. What do you do?

Discuss your role-playing with the other students in your group. Use the following questions to help you:

1. What information do you have to find out for your job?

2. How will you ask your boss to help you?

3. What will you do if your boss is out of the office?

Remember

It's all right to ask your boss or a co-worker questions. Decide what information you need before you ask questions.

In this unit you learned about

- talking to your boss
- talking to a co-worker
- talking to customers
- listening
- asking questions

Answer the following questions about the unit. Write your answers on the lines.

1. What is good body language?

_____

_____

_____

_____

2. What does co-worker mean?

_____

_____

_____

3. How should you always talk to customers, even when they are being unfair?

_____

_____

_____

_____

4. What should you do if your boss praises your work?

_____

_____

_____

_____

5. How do you feel about your problem-solving skills when talking to people at work? Explain your feelings.

_____

_____

_____

_____

_____

_____

_____

_____

_____

_____

_____

Role play the following scene:

You have never used a fax machine before. Your boss asks you to fax a form to another restaurant. You have to ask your boss how to use the machine. Write about it.

_____

_____

_____

_____

_____

_____

_____

_____

_____

_____

_____

_____

Discuss your role-playing with other students in your group.

Journal

Think about what you learned in this unit.

1. This is what I learned about talking with different people at work.

_____
_____
_____
_____
_____

2. This is what I had problems learning in the unit.

_____
_____
_____

3. These are the communication skills I have to improve.

_____
_____
_____

4. This is how I will improve those communication skills.

_____
_____
_____

5. Which lesson in the unit helped you most to see Tommy's problem? Explain how this made you feel.

_____
_____
_____
_____
_____
_____

UNIT 5 MAKING JUDGMENTS AND DECISIONS

How do you handle peer pressure at work?
How do you deal with personal issues on your job?
How do you deal with change at work?

The lessons in this unit will help you learn how to handle making decisions at work.

- In **Lesson 19**, you'll meet Laura. You'll learn how Laura acts when a co-worker wants her to do something that is wrong.

- In **Lesson 20**, you'll find out how Laura handles a problem with one of her co-workers.

- In **Lesson 21**, you'll find out how Laura learns to handle a personal issue at work.

- In **Lesson 22**, you'll find out how Laura learns to make changes to do her job differently.

What do you know about making decisions at work?

_____

_____

19 Peer Pressure

Pizza Palace

Laura likes her new job at the "Pizza Palace." Most of the time she's a kitchen helper. Today her boss asked Laura to help deliver pizzas. Laura and Charlene, another delivery person, left the restaurant at noon. They each made two deliveries. Laura was on her way back to the "Pizza Palace" when she met Charlene.

"Where are you going in such a hurry?" Charlene asked.

"Back to 'Pizza Palace'," Laura said. "It's lunchtime. I have to work in the kitchen."

Charlene laughed. "Take your time. That's what the rest of us do on a delivery."

Laura kept on walking. "I really should get back to work, Charlene. I don't want to lose my job."

Charlene put her hand on Laura's shoulder. "Don't worry so much about losing your job. Worry more about losing your friends on the job. Remember, don't get back from a delivery too fast. It makes the rest of us look bad."

Laura looked at Charlene. She wasn't sure what to do.

1. Why does Laura want to get back to the "Pizza Palace" on time?

_____

2. Why doesn't Charlene want Laura to get back to her job on time?

_____

3. If you were Laura, what would you do? Why?

_____

_____

Discuss your answers with the other students in your group.

Thinking It Through

Charlene wants Laura to do something that is wrong. Laura isn't sure what to do. There is a way she can solve her problem.

- Laura has to **understand** her problem. She must learn that she shouldn't react to **peer pressure**. Peer pressure is following the way your friends think and act. Even though everyone at work may act a certain way, it doesn't mean that their actions are right. Laura can ask herself, "How can I say no to Charlene?"

- Laura can **plan** a way to **solve** her problem. She can **discuss** with a friend or co-worker how to say "no." She can **make a list** of possible responses to Charlene in a notepad. The next time Charlene asks Laura to do something that she thinks is wrong, Laura can say "no." Then she can explain to Charlene how she feels.

- Laura can **check** her plan and make sure she solved her problem.

- Laura can **review** what she learned about saying no under peer pressure.

Try This

Think about how Laura learned to deal with peer pressure. Then act out this scene:

> You're getting some supplies at work. Another co-worker is in the supply room. He tells you to take some of the supplies home with you. "Everyone does it," he says. "It makes up for our small paychecks." What should you do?

Discuss your role-playing with the other students in your group. Use the following questions to help you:

1. Would you take the supplies for your personal use? Explain.

2. What would you say to your co-worker?

3. What would you do if your boss heard the conversation?

Remember

Learn to say no when a co-worker wants you to act or think a certain way because "everyone else does." If you know it is wrong, don't be afraid to say no.

---

20 Problems on the Job

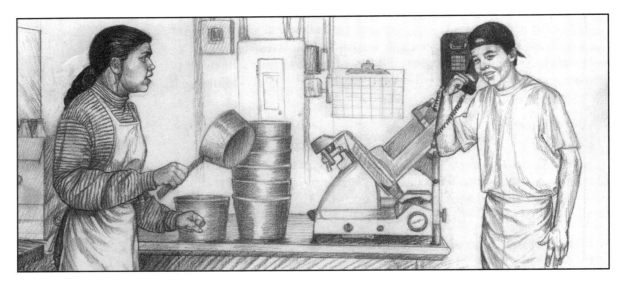

Laura wanted to do a good job at the "Pizza Palace." She had been working hard all afternoon in the kitchen. One of the kitchen workers wasn't doing his job. Kevin was supposed to help Laura fill the food orders. Instead, he talked on the telephone with his friends. Then he took a long work break. The restaurant was busy. So Laura was doing Kevin's job, too. "This isn't fair," Laura thought to herself. But Laura didn't say anything to Kevin. She felt herself becoming more and more angry. She felt like hitting Kevin. Finally, she threw a pot on the floor.

1. What problem did Laura have with Kevin?

_____

_____

2. How did Laura feel when she saw Kevin talking on the telephone?

_____

_____

3. If you were Laura, what would you have done?

_____

_____

Discuss your answers with the other students in your group.

Thinking It Through

If you're having problems with a co-worker or your boss, always talk about it. Never fight. Laura lost her temper because she was angry at Kevin. But there is a way she can deal with the problem.

- Laura has to **understand** her problem. Because Kevin isn't working, she's doing his job too.

- Laura can **plan** a way to **solve** her problem by **listing** the people she can talk to—Kevin and her boss. She should try to **work together** with Kevin. They can talk about the problem and find a way to handle it. If **talking** with Kevin doesn't work, then Laura should talk to her boss.

- Laura can **check** her plan and see if it worked.

- Laura can **review** what she learned about dealing with problems at work. Reviewing will help her deal better with similar problems in the future.

Try This

Think about how Laura handled her problem with Kevin. Then act out this scene:

> Your boss asks you to deliver a big package to a customer. She tells you to deliver the box in your car. You know that you can't use your car for business. How do you say no without being fired?

Discuss your role-playing with the other students in your group. Use the following questions to help you:

1. What will you say to your boss?

2. What will you do if your boss gets angry with you?

3. How will you do the job even if your boss gets angry? Explain.

┌─ **Remember** ─────────────────────────────────
│ If there's a problem at work, talk about it. Don't fight.
│ Never lose your temper with your co-worker, your boss,
│ or a customer.
└──

21 Personal Issues

Today Laura is taking food orders at "Pizza Palace." She knows she will be very busy writing orders in her notepad. She also knows that she must take her medicine on time every day. Laura's next work break is at 3:30 P.M. However, she has to take her medicine at 2:30 P.M. It's very important that Laura takes her pills at the right time. "If I leave before my work break, my boss will get angry," she thinks. Laura looked at her watch. It was 2:20 P.M. "What am I going to do?" she asked herself.

1. Why can't Laura take her pills during her work break at 3:30 P.M.?

_____

_____

2. Why doesn't Laura want to leave before her work break?

_____

_____

3. If you were Laura, what would you do?

_____

_____

Discuss you answers with the other students in your group.

Thinking It Through

Laura has a problem. She needs to take her medicine before her work break. There is a way she can help herself.

- Laura has to **understand** her problem. She can ask herself: "When do I have to take my pills? When is my next work break?"

- Laura can **plan** a way to **solve** her problem. She can **brainstorm** the names of people who can help her and can **talk** to them. She can make a list of the names in her notepad. Laura knows the best person to help her is her boss, Ms. Pèron. Before talking to her boss, Laura can **practice** what she will say to her. She can explain her problem.

- Laura can **check** her plan. Did her boss let Laura leave to take her pills? If her boss did, then Laura knows her plan worked.

- Laura can **review** what she learned about dealing with a personal problem at work. Reviewing will help her deal with similar problems in the future.

Try This

Think about how Laura handled her personal problem at work. Then act out this scene:

> You have to talk to your son's teacher at 4:30 P.M. To get to his school on time, you will have to leave work early. You have to ask your boss if you can leave work at 4:00 P.M. What do you do?

Discuss your role-playing with the other students in your group. Use the following questions to help you:

1. Why is leaving work early a problem?

2. Why is it important to talk to your boss?

3. What should you say to your boss? What body language should you use?

Remember

If you have a personal problem at work, talk to your boss about it. Plan ahead so that you know what you will say.

---

22 Change at Work

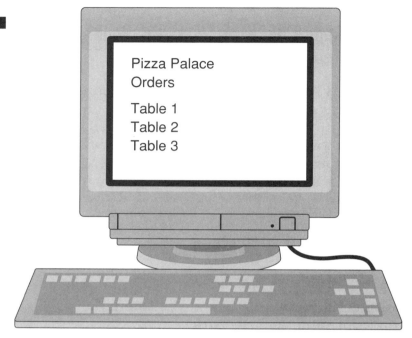

Pizza Palace
Orders

Table 1
Table 2
Table 3

Laura liked taking the customers' food orders at "Pizza Palace." It was more fun than working in the kitchen. Laura's job was going to change. She would have to put information about each food order into the computer. Laura didn't know how to use a computer. She felt nervous. Her boss, Ms. Pèron, said she would teach Laura what to do. "You're a good worker, Laura," Ms. Pèron said. "You'll learn how to do your job a new way, now."

Laura wasn't so sure. "Maybe I should go back to working in the kitchen," she thought.

1. How was Laura's job going to change?

_____

_____

2. Why was Laura nervous about her job now?

_____

_____

3. If you were Laura, what would you do?

_____

_____

Discuss you answers with the other students in your group.

Thinking It Through

Jobs can change in many ways. Sometimes you work for a new boss. Sometimes you have a new co-worker. Sometimes you are asked to do a different job even for a day. Laura had to learn how to do her job a new way. There is a way she can learn what to do.

- Laura has to **understand** her problem. She can ask herself, "How is my job going to change? What will I have to learn?"

- Laura can **plan** a way to **solve** her problem. Laura can **talk** to one of her co-workers who already uses the computer. Or Laura can learn computer skills from her boss. Laura can **practice** these skills until she feels confident.

- Laura can **check** her plan to see if it worked. She can ask herself "Did I learn how to use the computer for my job?"

- Laura can **review** what she learned about dealing with change at work.

Try This

Think about how Laura handled her problem. Then act out this scene:

> You have worked for your boss at the drugstore for two years. Now you have a new boss. He wants you to work a different shift at the store. What do you do?

Discuss your role-playing with the other students in your group. Use the following questions to help you:

1. What will you say to your new boss the first time you meet him?

2. What will you do when your new boss asks you to work a different shift?

3. How would you plan to solve this problem? Think about the choices you have. Explain why you like your choice best.

Remember

Your job can change in different ways. Don't be scared by the change. Don't quit your job. Instead, learn how to deal with the change.

UNIT 5 Review

In this unit you learned about

• handling peer pressure at work

• dealing with problems at work

• handling personal issues at work

• dealing with change on your job

Answer the following questions about the unit. Write your answers on the lines.

1. What is peer pressure?

_____

_____

_____

_____

2. If you have a problem with a co-worker, what is one thing you should never do?

_____

_____

_____

_____

3. If you have a personal problem to deal with at work, who is the best person to talk to?

_____

_____

_____

4. What are two ways in which your job can change?

_____

_____

_____

_____

5. What personal issues became a problem for you or a friend at work? Can you see another way either of you could have handled them?

_____

_____

_____

_____

_____

_____

_____

_____

_____

_____

Role play the following scene:

Your are a stock clerk at a store that sells running shoes. One of your friends is a stock clerk at the store, too. One afternoon you see her steal two pairs of shoes from the stockroom. What should you do? Write about it.

_____

_____

_____

_____

_____

_____

_____

_____

_____

_____

_____

_____

Discuss your role-playing with other students in your group.

Journal

Think about what you learned in this unit.

1. This is what I learned about making judgments and decisions at work.

_____

_____

_____

_____

2. This is what I'm still not sure about.

_____

_____

_____

_____

3. These are the skills I have to improve.

_____

_____

_____

_____

4. This is what I will do about handling peer pressure.

_____

_____

_____

_____

5. This is what I will do about handling a personal issue at work.

_____

_____

_____

_____

UNIT 6 MANAGING MONEY

Do you know what your net pay and your gross pay are?
How do you find out when you will be paid?
How do you spend your paycheck?

The lessons in this unit will help you learn about managing money.

- In **Lesson 23**, you'll meet Jamal. He works for the Parks Department. You'll find out how Jamal reads his pay stub.

- In **Lesson 24**, you'll learn about Jamal's payday.

- In **Lesson 25**, you'll learn how Jamal plans his work budget.

What do you know about how to read a pay stub?

_____

_____

_____

23 Reading a Pay Stub

Jamal had been working for the Parks Department for two weeks. Working outdoors was fun. So was getting a regular paycheck! Jamal figured out how much money he had earned in two weeks. He even knew how he would spend it. When Jamal received his pay envelope, he smiled and opened it right away. Then he stopped smiling—fast. Jamal looked at his name on the pay stub. The **pay stub** is a part of a paycheck. It showed important information about Jamal's **salary** or earnings.

"It's my name, all right," Jamal thought. "But what do all these numbers on this line mean? What's **gross pay** or **earnings**? What are these **taxes**? What does **total deductions** mean? Why is my check so much less than I thought it would be?" Jamal sighed. "I guess I can forget about fixing my car now."

1. Why do you think Jamal felt so happy when he received his pay envelope?

_____

_____

2. Why did Jamal feel so let down when he opened the pay envelope?

_____

_____

Discuss your answers with the other students in your group.

Thinking It Through

Here is Jamal's pay stub.

Company	Employee #	Date
Parks Department	200 38 0934	4/1/97

Gross	Fed.	State	Local	Net
$120.00	$18.04	$12.67	$6.34	$82.95

- To **understand** the numbers on his pay stub, Jamal needs to know what the following terms mean:

  1. **Gross pay** or **earnings** is a worker's earnings before taxes and other expenses are **deducted**, or taken away.

  2. **Taxes** is the money taken out of your paycheck by the government.

  3. **Total deductions** are the different taxes and other expenses such as insurance, retirement, or dues taken out.

  4. **Net earnings** are what a worker takes home after all taxes and other expenses have been deducted.

- To **plan** what he will earn in a month or year, Jamal can **write** down the amount of his net earnings. Then he can **use math skills** to get a monthly or a yearly salary. He can multiply his net earnings by the number of weeks he works to find his monthly or yearly salary.

- Jamal should **check** the meanings of the important words on his pay stub. If he has any questions, he can talk to his boss.

- Jamal can **review** what he learned about reading a pay stub.

Remember

It's important to understand what the numbers on your pay stub mean. If you any questions, talk to your boss.

---

24 Payday

Jamal has been working in Green Park all day. First he raked the leaves. Then he and the other workers painted an iron fence. It had been one week since his last payday. Jamal was looking forward to getting another paycheck at the end of the day. Jamal's boss, Mr. Allen had bad news. Jamal's next payday wasn't until the fifteenth of the month.

When Jamal went back to work, he talked to his friend José. "Waiting until the fifteenth of the month isn't so bad," Jamal said. "I worked a lot of hours."

"But don't forget, you were sick two days last week," José said. "We only get paid for the time we work. Didn't you know that?"

Jamal shook his head. "I do now. I'm glad someone told me."

SEPTEMBER						
S	M	T	W	T	F	S
	1	2	3	4	5	6
7	8	9	10	11	12	13
14	Payday (15)	16	17	18	19	20
21	22	23	24	25	26	27
28	29	Payday (30)				

1. When did Jamal think he would be paid?

_____

_____

2. Why would Jamal's paycheck be smaller than he expected?

_____

_____

3. If you were Jamal, how would you have found out information about your next payday?

_____

_____

_____

Discuss your answers with the other students in your group.

Thinking It Through

Jamal didn't have all the facts he needed to know. But Jamal can make sure he has the facts he needs in the future.

- Jamal can **understand** what he needs to know by asking himself two questions:

  1. When is my **payday**, the day of the month I will be paid?

  2. What is my **salary**, the money I make?

- Jamal can **plan** how to find out the answers. He can list the facts he needs to know:

  1. On what days of the month will I be paid?

  2. What is my **hourly wage**, the amount of money I get for an hour's work?

  3. How many hours did I work?

  4. Will I be paid for any sick days or holidays?

Then Jamal can **talk** to his boss and find out the answers to his questions.

- Jamal can **check** to make sure he has the facts he needs. If he needs more information he can talk to someone.

- Jamal can **review** what he learned about his payday and his paycheck.

Try This

Think about what you know about your payday. Then act out this scene:

> You've been working at your new job in a fast food restaurant for one week. You want to find out when your first payday is. You also want to know if you're paid for sick days. You decide to talk to your boss.

Discuss your role-playing with the other students in your group. Use the following questions to help you:

1. What questions will you ask your boss?

2. If your boss can't help you, what will you do?

┌─ **Remember** ─────────────────────────────
│ Find out when you will be paid each month. Write down or
│ circle the dates on a calendar to help manage your money.
└──

25 Budgeting

Today was payday for Jamal and the other Parks Department workers. Jamal quickly cashed his paycheck. He needed a heavy pair of shoes and a new sweatshirt for work. Now he could afford to buy them. On the way to the clothing store, Jamal bought a few CD's. "Do I have enough money to buy a new skateboard?" he thought. He spotted a great-looking T-shirt in a store window. "Hey, it won't hurt to look inside," Jamal thought. "I can get the work clothes later."

By the time Jamal left the store, he had bought two T-shirts and a new jacket. But he still didn't have his work clothes. Then Jamal checked his wallet. It was empty. He couldn't believe it. "How could I spend my whole paycheck so fast?" Jamal asked himself. "And what about the clothes I need for work?"

Weekly Expenses	
Bus fare	$15.00
Work clothes	?
Food	$25.00
Extras	?

1. What should Jamal have bought with his paycheck?

_____

_____

_____

2. If you were Jamal, what would you have done with your paycheck?

_____

_____

_____

Discuss your answers with the other students in your group.

Thinking It Through

Jamal didn't plan how he would spend his paycheck very well. There is a way he can help himself in the future.

- To **understand** how to plan his **expenses**, or what he spends his money on, Jamal can ask himself this question: "What are my most important work expenses each week?"

- To **plan**, Jamal needs to **write** a **budget**. A budget is a plan to show how much money you can spend on your expenses. Jamal can **list** his weekly work expenses on a piece of paper. Jamal can write down how much money he earns after taxes and other deductions. He can **compare** this amount with how much he has to spend. He can **decide** how much of his salary he will spend on each expense.

- To **check** his work budget, Jamal can follow it for one week and see if it works.

- Jamal can **review** what he learned about making up a work budget. That will help him manage his money better in the future.

Try This

Think about how Jamal spent his paycheck. Then act out this scene:

> You have just cashed your paycheck. You will need money for your bus fare to and from your job. You will also need some clothes for work. Your best friend tells you about a great CD sale. It's been a long time since you bought yourself a present.

Discuss your role-playing with the other students in your group. Use the following questions to help you:

1. What should you do as soon as you cash your paycheck?

2. Is saving your money for work expenses more important than buying something for yourself?

3. How will you use your paycheck?

Remember

Make up a budget to help you plan how you'll spend your paycheck.

UNIT 6 Review

In this unit you learned about

- reading a pay stub
- finding out when your payday is and how much you will be paid
- making up a work budget

Answer the following questions about the unit. Write your answers on the lines.

1. Why is the amount of your paycheck always less than the amount of money you earned ?

_____

_____

_____

2. What information is on a pay stub?

_____

_____

_____

_____

_____

_____

3. If you don't know when payday is, whom can you ask?

_____

_____

4. What are some important expenses in a work budget?

_____

_____

_____

_____

5. How has learning about managing money helped you the most? the least? Explain your answer.

_____

_____

_____

_____

_____

_____

_____

_____

_____

_____

Role play the following scene:

You have just received your paycheck. You expected to earn more money than you did. You don't understand why so much money was taken out of your paycheck. Write about it.

_____

_____

_____

_____

_____

_____

_____

_____

_____

_____

_____

Discuss this role-playing with other students in your group.

Journal

Think about what you learned in this unit.

1. This is what I learned about managing money.

_____

_____

_____

_____

2. This is what I'm still not sure about.

_____

_____

_____

_____

3. These are the skills about managing money that I have to improve.

_____

_____

_____

_____

4. This is how I will improve these money management skills.

_____

_____

_____

_____

5. This is how I will use these money management skills at work.

_____

_____

_____

_____

Glossary

A

application form a form filled in by someone looking for a job. This form asks for information about the person, including education and job history.

B

body language the way you look and act while you talk or listen during a conversation

budget a plan to pay for different expenses, such as food, clothing, and transportation

C

co-worker a person you work with on your job

D

deductions the amount of money taken out or withheld from a paycheck

digital clock a clock that shows time in numerals

dress code the special way of dressing for a certain job

E

employee a worker

employer a boss

expenses the different things you pay for that are related to your job (The most important expenses are food, clothing, and transportation.)

F

FICA stands for Federal Insurance Compensation Act. This act requires a boss to deduct money from a paycheck for federal taxes.

G

goals things that you work towards in life

gross earnings a worker's pay before any taxes and other expenses are deducted

H

hourly wage the amount of money paid to a worker for one hour's work

I

invoice a detailed list of goods and their prices

J

job duties all the different tasks you do at work

L

long-term goals a goal that takes a long time to reach (Long-term goals take a lot of hard work and planning.)

N

net earnings the amount of money a worker takes home after all taxes and other expenses such as insurance, retirement, and dues have been deducted

P

payday the day of the month when a worker is paid for his or her work

pay stub a part of a paycheck that shows important information about a worker's earnings, such as the worker's name, social security number, gross earnings, taxes, total deductions, and net earnings

peer pressure an unwritten way of thinking and acting that friends or co-workers want you to follow

personal schedule a time plan that tells you what to do and when to do it

R

route a way to get to a place

S

salary the amount of money an employee is paid for the work he or she does

short-term goals a goal that takes you a short time to reach

T

taxes a percentage of money deducted from a worker's paycheck by the government

time card a card that shows the exact time an employee arrives at work and leaves work

total deductions the sum of the different taxes and other expenses deducted from a paycheck

W

workday the number of hours an employee must work every day (A workday begins and ends at certain times, depending on the type of job and whether the work is part-time or full-time.)